It's time for bed.
What can Ned hear
on a noisy night?

Birds call in the dark.
It's a noisy night.

Birds call. Cars honk
on city streets.
It's a noisy night.

Birds call, and cars honk.
The crickets sing.
It's a noisy night.

Birds call, cars honk, and crickets sing. The cans clank. It's a noisy night.

Birds call, cars honk, and crickets sing. The cans clank, and a dog barks.

Ned is sleeping.
And it's a noisy night!

He Hears Noise

Talk to your partner about the noises
the boy hears. Which noises have you
heard?

 ## Night Sounds

Draw a picture of something you like to
hear at night. Write about
your picture.

I like to hear _____.

Sounds Around Us

GR D • Benchmark 6 • Lexile 190

Grade K • Unit 3 Week 2

www.mheonline.com

The **McGraw·Hill** Companies

ISBN-13 978-0-02-119434-6
MHID 0-02-119434-3

99701

EAN

9 780021 194346

K